Cycles of Life

Foreverness is in our eyes

Antonia Nilsson   Safwan Dahoul

Poetry   Painting

AuthorHouse™ UK
1663 Liberty Drive
Bloomington, IN 47403 USA
www.authorhouse.co.uk
UK TFN: 0800 0148641 (Toll Free inside the UK)
UK Local: 02036 956322 (+44 20 3695 6322 from outside the UK)

Because of the dynamic nature of the Internet, any web addresses or links contained in this book may have changed since publication and may no longer be valid. The views expressed in this work are solely those of the author and do not necessarily reflect the views of the publisher, and the publisher hereby disclaims any responsibility for them.

Adobe Stock images depicting people are used with their permission and for illustrative purposes only. Certain stock imagery © Adobe Stock.

This book is printed on acid-free paper.

ISBN: 979-8-8230-8624-0 (sc)
979-8-8230-8625-7 (e)

Library of Congress Control Number: 2024901774

Print information available on the last page.

Published by AuthorHouse 01/26/2024

authorHOUSE®

We dedicate this book to all the women who are suffering,
the ones who are silenced and overlooked, taken for granted, and undervalued.

Introduction

The reader is invited to a journey through cycles of life, visiting emotional and mental landscapes, looking at processes taking place on the earthly level, and casting a glance on the cosmological dimension. The journey begins with the creation of a personal space, an Eden in miniature, where creation is abundant, and voices are singing in harmony. After a while, unsettling ripples disturb the order of things, while dissonance infiltrates the inner space taking us by surprise.

The story is woven in a series of miniature narratives which form an odyssey. At first, the self looks at the world from a distance, trying to make sense of it all. After a while, she is caught in the violent process of transformation, forced to witness the changes that are taking place inside and outside. The veils of night flutter, disclosing hidden things, while the colourful curtains of day-to-day sensations act as lenses to her eyes.

There are two separated spaces engaged in a dialogue with each other. The first one is near us, in the here and now. The latter is the eternal, hidden beyond the transparent veils of consciousness. Celestial bodies are witnessing it and sometimes even intervening in the process.

The story resumes with a transcendence from one space to another. It's a symbolic death followed by a rebirth in a different context.

vi

Mirroring

The dialogue between the two sides of a coin
shows the opposites embedded in similarity,
flipping from the one to the other
each time we are looking at them.

As a new consciousness takes form,
the opposites find themselves integrated
into another whole.

Morning Light

The glow of completion
on the verge of newness
gives premonitions.
Beyond the scale of good or bad,
night lifts its veils of distance.

Butterfly Living

Cycles emerge from the void into the fabric of life.
The linen of here and now flutters in shades of blue.
Under sunrays and rain,
a metamorphosis of silk
crosses borders with ease.

The Jungle of Creation

Cascades of fertility
exceed all expectations
in the realm of manifestations
and its counterpart,
in the consciousness of humankind.
Auspicious skies have their elements tuned in,
reflecting themselves
in the well of the unconsciousness.

Benevolence

When borders become permeable to benevolence,
strips of brightness
transform themselves into elation,
knowing they are indispensable
for crops to become ripe.

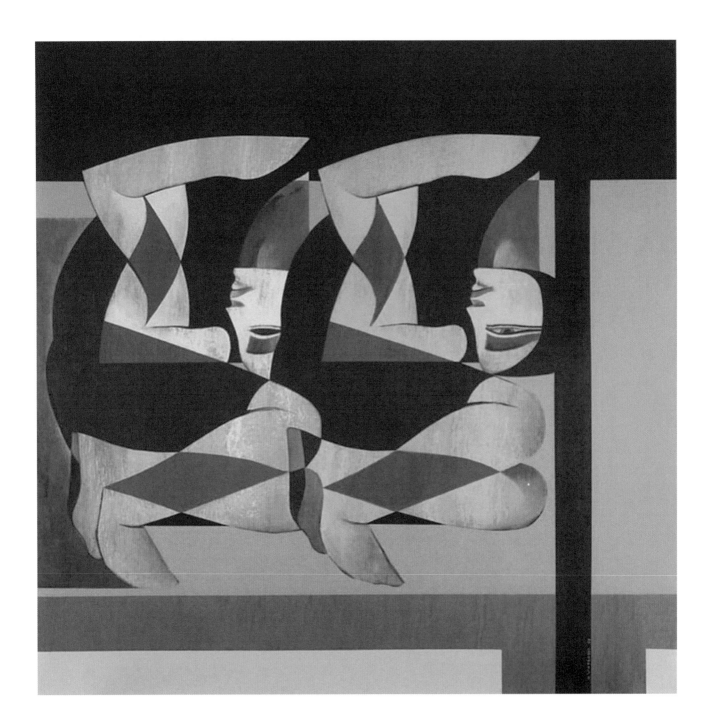

Strength

The fluxes of invisible matter oscillate in phase.
Full reciprocity
here and everywhere.
In this moment of unity,
the spectrum of nuances is omnipotent,
and strength is all what we breathe!

Indulgence

Exotic flavours of golden rains—
fruits falling ripe—
the quintessence of indulgence
gives playfulness to the lust of letting the hair down.
We take part in the decadence with a smile.

Moonlight

The golden night promises everything;
winds from the west bringing mists of a future,
nymphs singing in thousands of voices.
I love every single cell of it even if none is of
substance!

The Last Summer Day

A puff of clarity creates turbulence
in the air saturated of too much, too good.
Wings' flutter changes
around the permanence of a church roof
as we watch the summer playing itself
in the windows of the city before she leaves.

Actuality

Actuality punctuates the calmness of waters,
following their own ebb and flow.
The sunrise stands still, in limbo,
not knowing where to go
as circumstances
are tipping over the dark side
of the great expectations presumed.

The Star

Fixed by the precision of fatefulness,
the star cries to become a point of reference
for our own good.
As soon as it's acknowledged, grace emerges
on sea, on land, on air.
But we refused.

Puzzlewood

She told me,
"Beware the spells crossing murky waters,
mirroring themselves among shadows of bewitched
trees.
The answer isn't there for you,
no matter how sharp your look is."
But her warning was in vain.

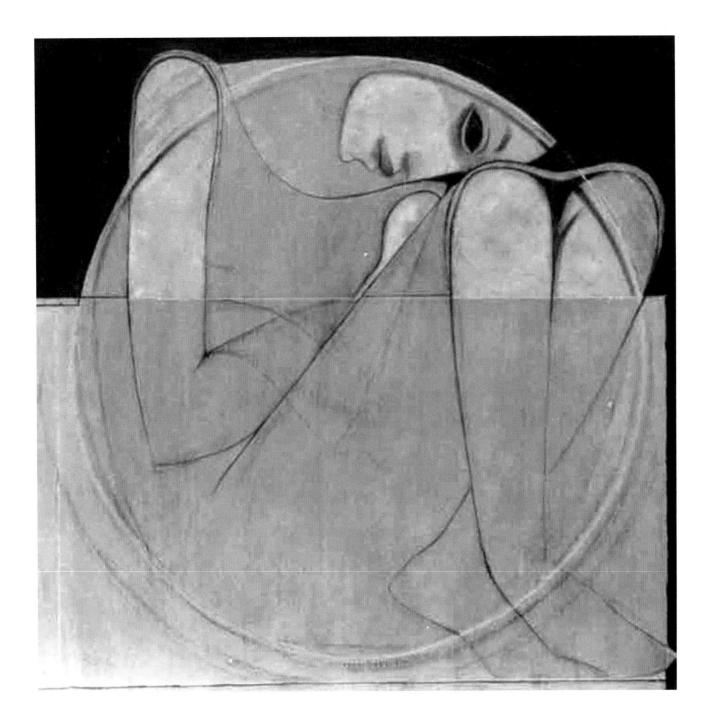

Ripples

Unsettling ripples disturb the fabric of now;
nothing big apart from a feeling of uneasiness.
So I calm down, counting arguments,
putting facts on the table.
No interpretations, just facts matter this time!

Next day arrives, loaded with a message,
short, clear, and heartbreaking.
Yesterday's ripples are now embodied in words.

Chord

Snapshots of life,
themes flashing
behind the ornaments
we've gathered as a shelter.
A chord
brings the seriousness to the foreground,
and its urgency becomes clear.

Loneliness

Separated from the vision of myself,

I'm out of reach.

Above my senses,

over my power of perception,

tattered flows of grief are the only ways in between.

Glowing Black

There are cracks
in the frozen hill of self-rigorousness.
On the mild side,
they run through the ice, melting dirty,
on the rebellious side,
clashing with adversity in avalanches.

The melting quality of progress is far from
immaculate.
Emerging from the black generator of colours,
it evolves self-contained,
while we fight changes,
from the fences we've built
of its shades.

The Circus

In the whiteness of intentions,
random raging radicalness
transforms itself into a collective race without aim.
The animal we train with our methods of pain
overpowers us on our own chessboard,
getting bigger than the scene
we made him to perform on.

Bad Omens

Bad omens are silent.
Watching the irreversibility approach us,
we seek reassurance in each other
until the facts get too near to be able to act.
We never broke that silent pact;
now they are multiplied.

The Tower

First is the tower landing-stroke side,

then comes the city.

A world dies melting in the waters of time living.

My point of reference goes with it.

I'm lost and found

in fragments,

still looking for ingredients

to build myself again.

Hiatus

Apocalyptic ebb
sucks out the contents of our lives,
all details defining ourselves,
the matters that count and all other things
rooted inside.

But changes occur ... in the back,
preparing themselves to crack
the steel surface of now.

Fear

Fear shoots.
Shockwaves, reflecting themselves
on blood vessel walls,
attain resonance in the eye of the storm,
the very place
where the vows are born.

The Survivor

I can't recall when it all happened;
neither can I see its order of magnitude.

Clinging to a fence, I was
in waiting for the final blow
that came ... unexpectedly,
even if it was expected.

Getting hit by splashes of life still warm,
watching them transforming themselves
into the unthinkable
I refuse to call it by name.

Worst of all,
How hard the last hopes were to kill!

Silence

The great silence
made me break my own windows towards life
just to realize
that it wasn't life, not the world
I was looking at.

Purgatory in Here and Now

Trapped.

No air.

Alone with thoughts, sickness, and stagnation.

Paralyzed by fear,

I can't live or die.

Just stay

till the poison is consumed

in the process of burning love.

Hopes, futures …

One day I can move a finger

and press the button on the remote control

I've been clinging to all this time.

The walls are gone.

Have they ever been there?

28

A Dress of Blood

I wear a dress of blood,
the one I've lost in the process of getting well.
Woven in the flesh of inadequacy,
pain, and shame,
it was part of me,
glazing pale.

Tightrope

I'm walking a tightrope and lose my composure,
vanishing a little every time that I fall,
deconstructing to fragments; I'm no longer
consistent,
losing the container that gives me a form.
Or maybe I'm testing my limits for freedom,
a questionable battle I fight all alone.
But in the process of being defeated,
I finally find a truth of my own.
Ironically, this isn't even a freedom
I'm ready to admit that I've won.

If Not Now, When?

If not now, when to open the dark-chocolate box,

swallowing all pieces

filled with the liquor of pain,

one by one,

in a head-on shock therapy,

performing exorcistic surgery

on something I adore.

Instead,

I make yet another plan

for how to avoid or postpone

building scaffolds around the mausoleum of

deceased deeds.

If not now, then when?

Dialysis Machine

Cleansing my breath, eyes, lips, hands,
whishes poisoning me.

Weeds of humiliation taking over
all the places I've been,
the people I've seen.
Dead or alive,
all the same.
Scenes repeated, variations inflicted
after a theme.
Trading dreams, integrity, means,
myself!

Remainings

A shiver drags me down the slippery stairs,
where dogs bark, voices mourn,
the pain takes me in whole.
I want him; I want him not.
In the end, nothing is left undone,
but I wake up *cured*.
With fresh winds fluttering my hair,
anchors of life flashing in a corner of an eye,
new worlds are born.

The Rebirth

Emerging
from the melting pot of memories resurfacing,
cooled down by the mists of now,
hope flies high.
The lace of white flags
witnesses in its vulnerability
in the void of strengths
hiding behind walls.

A Private Revolution

I have a private revolution
going on inside.
A deconstruction of dreams
imposed by circumstances,
the brutality of words
and the laziness in acting
against the demons with angelic faces
calling all my names.

Tracks

Ancient tracks, sucking sap,

singing the siren's song.

The blame's sighs of surrender to the order of things

claimed by the roots under my feet.

It's a denial of needs and a life seen as evil by an

act of security,

getting stuck in the inertia of things called "natural".

I need to be fierce to overcome its power of

conviction;

those weeds can't be dealt with once and for all.

It's a day-to-day chore to get the new path cleared.

Opening in Blue

Reflections of light
from inside out
draw shadows in sand as symbols.
Jewel drops sparkling of clarity
witness the growing of knowing within
all along unseen.

The Balancing Act

The balancing act between strengths
is a matter of delicate precision.
On the practical side,
a stable footprint is achieved at the expense of
idealism.
On the ethereal part,
love pushes us beyond the borders we've agreed as
feasible.
Fluxes from the higher spectrum
infiltrate the board itself,
transforming it into a runaway path.

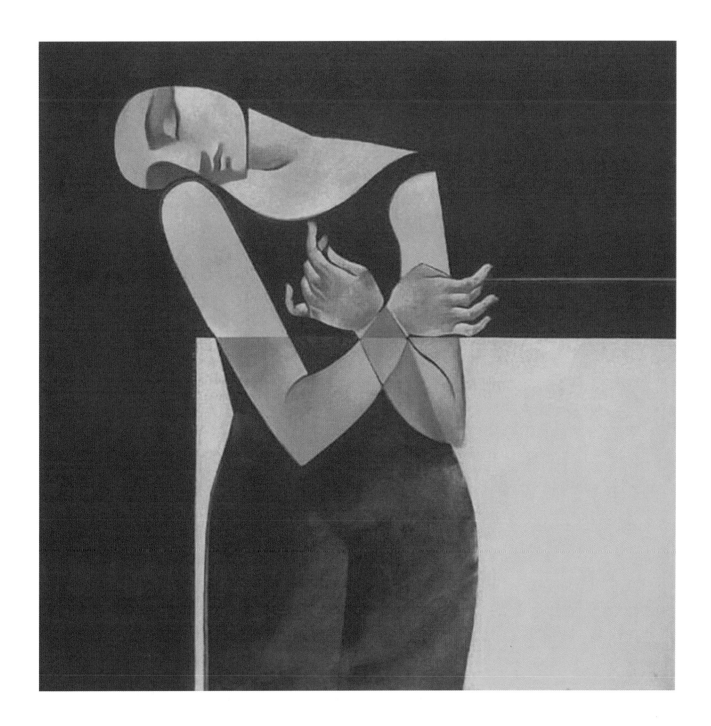

The Point of Golden Dust

Life is spilt
in the universe of ours.
Every opportunity
lost or taken
becomes a point in the multitude of intersections
having a charge attached,
a gravitational force towards the others.
One point in my field
is sparkling like gold.

Moon Mystery

The state of wonder calibrates the scales of distances,

making spaces to overlap.

Is this a free pass ticket?

By asking, we're already flying

through the newly opened gates.

Encounter

Crepuscular worlds breathe minutes, not hours.
I blush in an encounter
with the ephemeral,
a puff of life anew.

The Pink Moon

Under the water of time,

the pink moon

listens to the stories whispered

by the queen of shells

for millions of years.

The rusty space underneath is deteriorating

by our acid anxieties

under the secret penetration of rays

coming from days of the future.

Walking on Water

Seeing what isn't there
puts a stamp on my life forever.
And for me,
it will always exist.

47

A Vision is Gained

Fall in cloudy water.

No one's speaking anymore,

not even the voice of self-consciousness.

But the poignancy is spreading

larger, much larger than I thought.

And I move choreographed by this feeling.

I am the feeling, the movement, the water.

Except it's not water but sound

I'm immersed in,

and I could't see

as I'm waved in it,

a 3D,

no longer vanishing flat

in the fabric of normalcy.

Earthquake

A queer shake, a sharp squeak
find me reassured in my certainty of something
significant.
But cracks are running across the ground on which
I stand.
My convictions won't save me this time;
they're too harsh, too narrow, too strict.
We are the ones who judge.
We cast the spells; the ashes protect.

One Step Further Away

The irreversibility of this rupture insults me.
A glance was enough and can't be undone.
The uneasy facts,
the pretended sincerity deep down,
are echoing things I once said.

To find a shelter becomes insane.
So I put myself on fire
to burn on one stake with my faith.

Faith and I
We burned down to nothing,
and woke up from the narcosis of the soul
newly germinated—
lush, green, volatile, serene.
The picture of tomorrow
is still shaking in the mirror of today.
Life can be seen
shifting in its structures of resistance.

After Fire

It's a vulnerable episode.
Don't drown it in the details
of a day-to-day life!
The ground trembles, watching
how embryos of lives are growing in its fabric.
In normal circumstances,
they wouldn't stand a chance,
but things are different now.
Life counts no matter how small!

Love

To achieve capital changes,
love needs to penetrate at depth
to access and erase the script
cascading between generations.
When successful,
it's done in one stroke,
and it's permanent.

At the Border

You stand on the edge between here and everywhere,

now and forever,

a poetic expression of a life in beauty.

Spilled trust shades the moonlight over you,

while ashes protect

your soon-arriving passage.

Zoom Out

Zoom out,
leaving behind
the claustrophobic insignificance
of being biologically constrained.

At a different scale,
souls form a pattern.

By becoming one
with the purity acquired,
you will access the secrets.

The Ladder of Jacob

Blushing shyness, blushing love,

thread lightly please, within the space

where the shadow part of light is white.

Let's become one with those who climb

the ladder of air!

This way, we are protected from Icarus's spell.

Have fate, my love,

we are allowed this time.

We *are* allowed.

Dissociation

Sinking into the waters of temporality,
our lives dissolve themselves
in all the colours we've ever worn,
the blood serving us no more.
We turn apart into ribbons of narratives,
while the pillars of resistance
dissociate under the reflection
of what we once considered ephemeral.

Transcendence

All symbols of power are off.

No scale is on duty ...

Nor good or bad,

high or low,

appropriate or not,

stellar constellations say go,

right through things,

unprecedented now.

Far Away in Another Cosmos

Our freedom makes us gravitate around the essential.

Apart from it,

we can cross the sky among stars in elliptical paths.

By making the focal point our reference, it's getting effortless.

Antonia Nilsson is a poet and novelist who loves art. She collaborates with several artists all over the world and writes poems inspired by the atmosphere and ideas that emerge from the meeting between writing and visual arts. Recently at the art Biennale in Venice she collaborated with the Swedish artist Ragnhild Lunden.

Antonia aims to turn poetry into a way of living together with dance, performance, and music. So also, for this book. The poems are partly autobiographical showing mental landscapes and processes in flux between the material world and the realm of subconsciousness. It addresses ways in which a person can give painful and traumatic events a meaning. In her poems Antonia addresses the deep humbleness, humanity, and divinity in one that only arts can address.

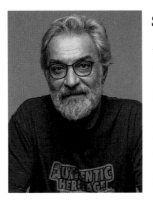

Safwan Dahoul is one of the foremost painters in the Arab world. He has repeatedly demonstrated how contemporary modes of figuration can describe the psychic terrain of a region that is in constant flux.

He is known for his melancholic and monochromatic works that present influences from the Cubist style to Assyrian and Pharaonic art.

The dream series explore the physical and psychological effects of alienation, solitude and longing that punctuate the human experience at various stages in life.

Partly autobiographical, this seminal body of work uses the formal properties of painting to recreate the subconscious sense of enclosure that surfaces during times of Chrysis.

The artists recuring female protagonist facilitates this visceral experience trough her contorted body, often vacant eyes, and minimized yet monumental physicality.

Printed in the United States
by Baker & Taylor Publisher Services